Globalization is Complex

How the World is Changing

Written by:

Dr. David K. Ewen

Ambassador Professor
Global Studies University
Enterprise College

ISBN: 9798321920893
Imprint: Independently published by Enterprise College

Cover art by Kalen Emsley via Unsplash

Dr. David K. Ewen

www.GlobalStudiesUniversity.com

www.EnterpriseCollege.org

www.Bravehearted413.com

Table of Contents

About the Book

How does globalization, a dynamic and multifaceted process that weaves together economies, cultures, and societies around the globe, create such a complex tapestry of global interdependence? Is it not fascinating how this web extends far beyond mere trade, encompassing the flow of ideas, technologies, and people, thereby contributing to the ever-evolving global narrative? What makes understanding globalization such a challenging endeavor, considering it is shaped by and shapes a myriad of factors, from economic policies and cultural norms to technological advancements and environmental considerations?

At the heart of globalization's complexity, isn't it the economic interdependence of nations that stands out? How has the global economy, increasingly interconnected through trade agreements and multinational corporations, managed to blur the lines between domestic and international markets so effectively? Can the integration that has led to unprecedented economic growth and development, lifting millions out of poverty, also be the very thing that makes us vulnerable to economic turmoil across the globe, as seen in recent global financial crises? What does it take to balance the benefits of economic integration with the need for stability and resilience against such shocks?

6 - Globalization is Complex

Culturally, how has globalization facilitated an exchange of ideas and values that enriches and challenges traditional ways of life simultaneously? In an age where digital media and the Internet enable cultures to share their essence with a global audience, fostering appreciation for the world's diversity, how do we address the tensions that arise from cultural homogenization and the erosion of local identities? What does the dialogue between the global and the local, between preserving one's cultural heritage and embracing new influences, truly entail?

In this ever-changing world, does globalization not remain a complex phenomenon that defies simple explanations or solutions? Does it not embody the tensions between the global and the local, the individual and the collective, offering opportunities for progress while presenting challenges of inequity? As we navigate the 21st century, how crucial is it that we strive for a nuanced understanding of globalization's multifaceted impacts and engage in collective efforts to shape a future that is equitable, sustainable, and inclusive for all?

Let's find out.

About the Author

Dr. David K. Ewen, an esteemed figure in the realm of global studies and education, stands as a beacon of knowledge and innovation in understanding the intricacies of our interconnected world. As the president and founder of Global Studies University and Enterprise College, Dr. Ewen has embarked on a remarkable journey since the inception of his company in 1994. His path has been paved with the pursuit of understanding the changing dynamics of people, economies, technologies, and cultures across the globe. This quest has not only fueled his passion but also enabled him to discern patterns that offer a glimpse into the future's fabric.

Dr. Ewen's educational background, with a Master of Education (M.Ed.) degree in management and a Doctor of Education (Ed.D.) degree in global studies, provides a solid foundation for his exploration and research into global trends. His academic credentials underscore a deep commitment to education and a keen insight into global affairs, which have been instrumental in his ability to lead and innovate in the field of global studies.

In his endeavors, Dr. Ewen has not worked in isolation. Recognizing the value of collaboration and diverse perspectives, he has teamed up with global professionals from academia across various regions of the world, including Asia, the Middle East, Europe, the United States, and South America. This collaborative approach has enriched his research and insights, bringing a wealth of knowledge and experience to the table. Together, they have delved into the complexities of globalization, examining how the forces of change affect societies, economies, and cultures worldwide.

Through his extensive research and collaboration, Dr. Ewen has uncovered the changing nature of our world. He has observed firsthand how shifts in economic paradigms, technological advancements, and cultural dynamics influence global interactions and interdependencies. His work has led to the discovery of patterns that help predict future trends, offering valuable insights for academics, policymakers, businesses, and individuals alike. These patterns serve as a roadmap, guiding stakeholders through the complexities of globalization and helping them to navigate the challenges and opportunities that lie ahead.

Dr. Ewen's contributions extend beyond academic research and collaboration. As a visionary leader, he has played a pivotal role in shaping the curriculum and initiatives at Global Studies University and Enterprise College. His leadership has ensured that the institution remains at the forefront of global education, preparing students to thrive in an increasingly interconnected and rapidly changing world. Under his guidance, the university and college have become incubators for future leaders, equipped with the knowledge and skills to make meaningful contributions to global society.

Chapter 1: Navigating the Complexities of Globalization

Globalization has been one of the defining phenomena of the late 20th and early 21st centuries, reshaping the world in profound ways. It has facilitated an unprecedented level of integration across economic, political, and cultural boundaries, fundamentally altering how nations and individuals interact. This integration has yielded considerable benefits, notably in how it has driven economic growth, lifted millions out of poverty, and facilitated a rich exchange of cultures and ideas across the globe. However, the journey through globalization has not been without its turbulence. It has introduced complex challenges that have sparked significant debate and backlash in various quarters, reflecting the multifaceted impact of this global phenomenon.

One of the most celebrated aspects of globalization is its economic impact. By opening up markets and encouraging trade and investment across borders, globalization has spurred economic growth, created jobs, and led to the development of a more interconnected and efficient global economy. Countries have been able to specialize in areas where they have a competitive advantage, leading to better products and services at lower costs. This economic dynamism has been instrumental in lifting countries out of poverty, bringing unprecedented prosperity to many parts of the world that were previously marginalized in the global economy.

Beyond the economic sphere, globalization has had a profound cultural impact. It has facilitated the movement of people on an unprecedented scale, leading to vibrant exchanges of culture, customs, and perspectives. Food, music, art, and fashion from various corners of the world have found new audiences globally, enriching people's lives and fostering a greater understanding and tolerance of diverse cultures. This cultural blending has been one of the more positive narratives of globalization, highlighting its capacity to bring humanity closer together.

However, the very interconnectedness that defines globalization also means that economic, political, or social disturbances in one region can have wide-reaching effects. The global financial crisis of 2008 is a stark reminder of how interconnected the world's economies are and how vulnerabilities can quickly proliferate across borders. Moreover, this interdependence has introduced complexities in managing global economic stability, requiring coordinated efforts that are often challenging to achieve due to divergent national interests.

Globalization has also been a double-edged sword in the realm of security. The ease of movement across borders and the proliferation of digital communication platforms have empowered nonstate actors, including terrorist groups and transnational criminal organizations. These entities exploit the open, interconnected nature of the globalized world to operate across national boundaries, presenting new security challenges that are difficult to address within the traditional frameworks of national defense.

Perhaps one of the most contentious aspects of globalization is its uneven distribution of benefits. While some regions and sectors have thrived, others have felt left behind or exposed to the negative impacts of open markets, such as job losses in industries that face competition from imports. This has led to growing economic disparity and contributed to a sense of injustice and frustration among those who perceive themselves as losers in the globalized economy. Such sentiments have fueled a backlash against globalization in various countries, manifesting in protectionist policies, a resurgence of nationalism, and skepticism towards international institutions and agreements.

This backlash is intertwined with significant shifts in global politics. Traditional economic and political alliances are being reevaluated, and there is a noticeable move towards unilateralism in some quarters. The political discourse is increasingly framed around identity and sovereignty, challenging the multilateral approach that has underpinned international relations in the post-

World War II era. Additionally, the rise of emerging powers like China is reshaping the global order, leading to a realignment of international relations and challenging the dominance of established powers like the United States.

The complexity of globalization necessitates nuanced and flexible approaches to governance, both at the national and international levels. It underscores the need for policies that not only harness the benefits of globalization but also mitigate its downsides. This includes ensuring that the gains from globalization are more equitably distributed and that there are robust systems in place to manage the economic, security, and cultural challenges it presents.

Chapter 2: Economic and Financial Benefits

The transformative power of globalization on the world economy is profound and far-reaching, reshaping economic landscapes across the globe. Through the facilitation of increased trade and financial exchanges, globalization has become a driving force behind strong economic growth, pulling numerous countries out of the clutches of poverty. This wave of economic integration has ushered in an era where resources are distributed more efficiently across borders, technological innovations are shared more widely, and employment opportunities are created in diverse sectors and regions, contributing to a more dynamic global economy.

The essence of globalization in the economic sphere is the creation of a tightly knit fabric of global trade and investment flows, where countries are more interconnected than ever before. This interconnectedness is not just a matter of increased economic activity but represents a fundamental shift in how economies operate and interact on a global scale. The ease with which goods, services, capital, and labor move across borders has led to economies that are not only interdependent but also more susceptible to influences from external markets and global trends.

One of the critical aspects of this global economic integration is the way it has facilitated a more efficient distribution of resources. Countries can now specialize in producing goods and services where they have a competitive advantage, leading to improvements in productivity and efficiency. This specialization is supported by the global trade system, which allows for the exchange of these goods and services on an international scale, ensuring that resources are used where they can generate the most value.

Moreover, globalization has been a catalyst for the spread of technological innovations. Technologies developed in one part of the world are quickly adopted in others, driving improvements in productivity and facilitating the emergence of new industries and jobs. This rapid dissemination of technology has also played a critical role in leveling the playing field, allowing emerging economies to leapfrog development stages that more advanced economies had to pass through more gradually.

The creation of jobs across borders is another testament to the impact of globalization on the world economy. As companies expand their operations internationally, they generate employment opportunities in various countries, contributing to economic growth and development. These opportunities are not limited to multinational corporations but also include small and medium-sized enterprises that are now able to access global markets more easily than ever before.

However, the high degree of economic interconnectedness brought about by globalization also means that the global economy is more interlinked, making it susceptible to the ripple effects of developments in one market or region. Economic crises, policy changes, or significant events in one country can have immediate and far-reaching impacts on others, as seen in the global financial crisis of 2008. This interdependence underscores the importance of coordination and cooperation among countries to manage global economic vulnerabilities and ensure stable and sustainable growth.

In summary, globalization has significantly impacted the world economy, driving growth, enhancing efficiency, and fostering the spread of innovation. It has transformed how economies operate, making them more interconnected and interdependent. While this brings numerous benefits, it also requires a greater focus on managing the challenges that come with such close economic ties.

Chapter 3: Cultural Benefits

Globalization's reach extends far beyond the realms of economics and politics, deeply influencing the cultural tapestry of societies worldwide. This phenomenon has facilitated the movement of people across borders on an unprecedented scale, catalyzing significant exchanges of culture, customs, and perspectives. As individuals from diverse backgrounds interact, their cultural traditions, values, and practices intermingle, leading to a rich mosaic of global culture that is continuously evolving. This blending of cultures enriches societies by broadening worldviews, diversifying artistic expressions, and expanding culinary horizons, among other benefits.

The movement of people—whether for work, education, or as part of migration patterns—serves as a primary conduit for these cultural exchanges. As people settle in new countries, they bring with them the customs and traditions of their homelands, introducing their new communities to different ways of life. This exchange is bidirectional; not only do immigrants adopt aspects of their host country's culture, but they also leave an indelible mark on it, weaving their cultural heritage into the fabric of their new home. The result is a society that is more culturally rich and diverse, where traditional distinctions blur, and new hybrid identities emerge.

One of the most visible signs of this cultural blending is in the diversification of cuisines worldwide. Globalization has made it possible for people to enjoy a vast array of foods from different cultures in their local communities. From the proliferation of sushi restaurants in cities far from Japan to the popularity of Italian pizzerias in countries around the globe, the culinary landscape has been transformed by global influences. This culinary diversity is not just about the enjoyment of new flavors but also signifies a deeper appreciation and understanding of different cultures through their food traditions.

The arts and cultural products have similarly benefited from globalization. The global exchange of films, music, literature, and art has exposed people to creative expressions from around the world, enriching the global cultural repository. Artists are inspired by traditions and techniques from other cultures, leading to innovative works that transcend traditional cultural boundaries. Moreover, the global circulation of cultural products fosters a shared experience among people of different backgrounds, promoting mutual understanding and empathy.

The enrichment of societies through cultural exchanges goes beyond the tangible aspects of food and art, deeply influencing people's perspectives and attitudes. Exposure to different cultures broadens individuals' worldviews, helping them appreciate the diversity of human experience and fostering a more inclusive and tolerant society. It challenges preconceived notions and stereotypes, encouraging people to look beyond their cultural confines and understand the value of different perspectives.

In essence, the cultural impact of globalization is profound and multifaceted, touching every aspect of human society. It has not only facilitated the exchange of cultural goods and practices but has also played a crucial role in shaping identities, attitudes, and social norms. Through this continuous exchange, cultures evolve, societies become more diverse and inclusive, and individuals gain a broader understanding of the world and their place within it. The cultural dimension of globalization illustrates how interconnected and interdependent the world has become, highlighting the importance of cultural exchange in fostering global understanding and cooperation.

Chapter 4: The Ripple Effects of Economic Interconnection

The interconnectedness brought about by globalization has undeniably transformed the global economy, creating a network of economic ties that span continents. This interconnection has facilitated numerous benefits, including increased trade, financial flows, and the spread of technology, which in turn have contributed to economic growth and development across the world. However, this deeply intertwined economic landscape also comes with its vulnerabilities. One of the most significant implications of this interconnectedness is the potential for economic challenges in one part of the world to quickly cascade through the global economy, affecting countries far removed from the original source of turmoil.

The global financial crisis of 2008 serves as a stark reminder of how economic disturbances can reverberate globally. What began as a crisis in the United States housing market quickly escalated into a global economic downturn, affecting financial markets, economies, and livelihoods around the world. This crisis underscored the degree to which global economies are linked and how issues in one significant market can have far-reaching effects, spreading quickly beyond national borders through the channels of global trade and finance.

This vulnerability of the global economy to localized economic challenges highlights the critical need for robust global economic policies and cooperation among nations. Managing and mitigating potential crises in such an interconnected environment require coordinated efforts and policies that transcend national interests. It calls for international cooperation among governments, financial institutions, and regulatory bodies to develop and implement policies that can prevent localized economic problems from escalating into global crises.

The importance of global economic cooperation is not just about crisis management; it also involves preventive measures such as establishing international financial regulations, monitoring global economic indicators to identify potential risks, and ensuring that there are mechanisms in place for quick and effective response to economic shocks. This cooperation can take many forms, including bilateral agreements, multilateral forums like the Group of Twenty (G20) or international institutions like the International Monetary Fund (IMF) and the World Bank, which play a crucial role in stabilizing the global economy.

Moreover, this situation calls for a reevaluation of global economic governance structures to ensure they are equipped to handle the complexities of the interconnected global economy. This involves not only strengthening existing institutions but also possibly reimagining international economic cooperation to address the challenges of the 21st century. It requires a commitment to collective action and shared responsibility, recognizing that in an interconnected world, the economic fortunes of nations are inextricably linked.

In conclusion, while the interconnectedness of the global economy has facilitated unprecedented levels of economic growth and development, it also presents significant challenges. The potential for localized economic challenges to have global repercussions necessitates a concerted effort towards robust global economic policies and cooperation. By working together, countries can safeguard against the vulnerabilities inherent in an interconnected global economy, ensuring a more stable and prosperous future for all.

Chapter 5: Threats from Non-State Actors

The forces of globalization, while fostering economic growth and cultural exchange, have also introduced complex security challenges by enabling the rise of nonstate actors such as terrorist groups. The very attributes of globalization that facilitate the free flow of goods, services, and information across borders also provide these groups with unprecedented opportunities to expand their reach and influence. The ease with which they can now operate across national boundaries presents a new type of threat, one that traditional defense mechanisms, primarily designed to counter threats from other nation-states, are often ill-prepared to address.

This evolution of security threats reflects a broader shift in the nature of global conflicts and challenges. Nonstate actors, leveraging global communication networks and financial systems, can orchestrate and execute operations that have far-reaching impacts, transcending the geographic confines that typically restrict the activities of more traditional threats. Their ability to mobilize, recruit, and disseminate propaganda globally, often with surprising speed and efficiency, adds a layer of complexity to the security landscape that many nations find challenging to navigate.

The rise of these groups and the transnational nature of their operations underscore the limitations of relying solely on national defense strategies. Traditional defense measures, while still critical, must be complemented by more nuanced approaches that address the unique characteristics of these non-state actors. This situation calls for a paradigm shift in how security threats are approached, moving toward strategies that are as agile and interconnected as the networks they aim to counter.

International cooperation emerges as a crucial element in this new security paradigm. Given that these threats do not respect national borders, efforts to combat them cannot be confined within the boundaries of any single country. Instead, there must be a concerted, collaborative effort among nations to share intelligence, coordinate responses, and dismantle the networks that support these groups. This requires not only cooperation among military and intelligence agencies but also among financial institutions, technology companies, and civil society organizations, all of which play a role in either inadvertently facilitating or combating the activities of these groups.

Moreover, innovative strategies are essential to address the root causes of terrorism and extremism, which often lie in political, economic, and social grievances. Efforts must therefore extend beyond military and security measures to include diplomatic initiatives, economic development programs, and efforts to promote social cohesion and inclusivity. By addressing the underlying issues that fuel the rise of nonstate actors, the international community can undermine their appeal and support base, making it more difficult for them to operate.

In essence, the globalized world demands a security approach that is as interconnected and multifaceted as the threats it faces. Combating the rise of nonstate actors requires more than just national defense strategies; it necessitates a global response that leverages international cooperation and innovative approaches to address the complex web of issues underlying global security challenges. This comprehensive approach is not only essential for neutralizing current threats but also for building a more secure and stable international order that can effectively manage the challenges of the 21st century.

Chapter 6: Uneven Distribution of Benefits

Globalization, for all its capacity to drive economic growth and foster interconnectedness across the globe, has also laid bare significant disparities in how its benefits have been apportioned. While certain regions and sectors have surged ahead, reaping the rewards of expanded trade, investment, and technological advancements, others have found themselves sidelined, exacerbating existing economic divides and fostering new ones. This uneven distribution of globalization's gains has not only heightened economic disparity but has also sown seeds of discontent among those who feel they have been left out of the narrative of global progress.

The stark contrast between winners and losers in the global economy has become a source of friction, sparking debates about the nature of globalization and its impacts. In regions where industries have declined or where jobs have been lost to more competitive markets abroad, there is a growing sentiment that the global economic playing field is far from level. Similarly, in countries that have not experienced the expected economic lift from globalization, there is frustration over unfulfilled promises of prosperity. This dissatisfaction has manifested in various forms, from protests against international trade agreements to the resurgence of protectionist policies aimed at safeguarding domestic industries from global competition.

The backlash against globalization can, in part, be attributed to the perception that it serves the interests of a global elite at the expense of the broader population. Critics argue that while multinational corporations and certain economies benefit from the removal of trade barriers and the integration of global markets, the resulting job displacement and environmental impacts disproportionately affect the most vulnerable. This has led to calls for a reassessment of how the benefits of globalization are distributed and for the implementation of policies that ensure more equitable growth.

Addressing these concerns requires a multifaceted approach that acknowledges the complexities of the global economy. Proposals for mitigating the negative impacts of globalization include strengthening social safety nets to support those affected by economic transitions, investing in education and training programs to equip workers with skills relevant to the changing economy, and implementing fair trade practices that protect workers and the environment. Additionally, there is a growing recognition of the need for international cooperation to address the challenges of globalization, ensuring that policies are not just aimed at protecting domestic interests but also at fostering a more inclusive and sustainable global economic system.

Efforts to promote equitable growth also involve rethinking the role of international institutions and agreements in governing global economic activity. By ensuring that these frameworks consider the needs of all stakeholders, including developing countries and marginalized communities, it is possible to create a more balanced approach to globalization. This includes not only addressing economic disparities but also considering the social and environmental dimensions of global development.

In essence, while globalization has the potential to continue driving global progress, its future trajectory will likely be shaped by how effectively the international community addresses the issue of uneven benefits. Recognizing the legitimate concerns of those who feel left behind and taking concrete steps to ensure that globalization leads to inclusive and sustainable growth are critical challenges that need to be met.

Chapter 7: The Backlash Against Globalization

In the landscape of global politics, recent years have witnessed a pronounced shift towards nationalist and unilateralist tendencies in several countries. This movement, in many ways, represents a backlash against the forces of globalization, which, despite bringing about significant economic and cultural integration, have also been perceived to contribute to economic disparities and a loss of national identity. Countries that once championed the ideals of multilateralism and international cooperation are increasingly adopting policies that prioritize national interests, often at the expense of global collaboration. This trend has significant ramifications for global governance and the collective capacity to tackle international challenges, from climate change to security threats and economic crises.

The roots of this shift are multifaceted, but a common thread is the growing dissatisfaction among populations who feel left behind by globalization. The perception that the benefits of a globally integrated economy have been unevenly distributed has fueled nationalist sentiments, with political leaders leveraging these feelings to gain support for policies that promise to put their country first. These policies often manifest in the form of trade protectionism, strict immigration controls, and a reluctance to commit to international agreements that are seen as compromising national sovereignty.

As countries turn inward, the fabric of international cooperation begins to fray. The institutions and frameworks that have underpinned the global order post-World War II, designed to facilitate cooperation and prevent conflict, are finding it increasingly difficult to function effectively. When unilateral actions replace collective decision-making, addressing global issues becomes a Herculean task. Challenges that inherently require international collaboration, such as climate change, pandemics, and transnational terrorism, cannot be effectively addressed by nations acting alone. The erosion of multilateralism undermines the ability of the international community to respond to these challenges in a unified and effective manner.

Complicating the political landscape further is the resurgence of identity-based conflicts, which have begun to eclipse traditional economic divides of left and right. Political discourse is increasingly dominated by issues of national identity, culture, and sovereignty, which, while important, often distract from pressing global challenges that require immediate attention. This shift has made political cooperation more challenging, not just internationally but within countries as well. The polarized nature of these debates creates an environment where compromise is difficult, and the common ground is hard to find.

The consequences of this trend towards nationalism and unilateralism are far-reaching. They signal a potential reordering of the international system, where the principles of cooperation and collective action give way to a more fragmented and competitive geopolitical environment. This not only poses a threat to global stability but also impedes progress on issues of global concern. For international challenges to be effectively addressed, a renewed commitment to multilateralism and global cooperation is essential.

However, forging this path requires acknowledging and addressing the legitimate concerns that have fueled the rise of nationalism. It involves creating a more inclusive form of globalization that equitably distributes its benefits, respects national identities, and strengthens the social compact within and among nations.

Chapter 8: Shifting Global Dynamics

The geopolitical landscape is undergoing a significant transformation as the global influence of traditional powers, epitomized by the United States, evolves in the face of emerging challenges. China's ascent, in particular, exemplifies this shift, marking a profound change in the balance of power that has defined international relations and governance structures since the end of World War II. These developments signal a departure from a world order that has been largely shaped by American values and priorities, towards one that is increasingly multipolar and complex. This evolution has profound implications for international organizations and regimes, highlighting the necessity for these institutions to adapt in order to remain relevant and effective in the face of contemporary global challenges.

The post-World War II era was characterized by the establishment of a broad array of international organizations and agreements designed to facilitate cooperation, prevent conflict, and promote prosperity. These institutions were largely founded on principles and norms that reflected the interests and values of Western powers, with the United States playing a leading role. However, as the global center of gravity shifts, these institutions are being challenged to accommodate the interests and perspectives of a more diverse set of actors, particularly rising powers like China that seek a greater role in shaping international norms and policies.

China's rise is not merely an economic or military phenomenon; it also entails a bid for greater influence over the architecture of global governance. This includes a push for reforms in existing institutions, such as the United Nations and the World Bank, as well as the creation of new mechanisms and forums where emerging powers have a more significant voice. These efforts reflect not only China's aspirations to reflect its status as a global power but also a broader demand for a more inclusive and equitable international system that takes into account the interests of a wider array of states, especially those from the Global South.

This transition presents both challenges and opportunities for the international community. On one hand, the inclusion of new perspectives and priorities can enrich the global governance system, making it more representative of the world it seeks to organize and regulate. On the other hand, diverging interests and values may complicate the process of reaching consensus on how to address global issues, from climate change and economic instability to security threats and human rights. The challenge, therefore, lies in finding ways to accommodate these diverse interests while maintaining the capacity for effective collective action.

The need for global institutions to adapt in response to these changes is clear. This adaptation may involve reforms to ensure more equitable representation and decision-making processes, the development of new norms and standards that reflect the realities of a multipolar world, and enhanced mechanisms for dialogue and cooperation among a broader set of stakeholders. Moreover, these institutions must become more agile and responsive to emerging global challenges, many of which, such as cybersecurity threats and the impacts of artificial intelligence on society, were unforeseen when these organizations were originally established.

In essence, the changing dynamics of global power underscores the need for a reinvigorated and reimagined system of international governance. By embracing inclusivity and leveraging the strengths and perspectives of both traditional and emerging powers, global institutions can better address the complex challenges of the 21st century. This evolution towards a more diversified and dynamic form of global governance is not only inevitable but also necessary for building a more stable, prosperous, and equitable world.

Chapter 9: The Path Forward

Effective global governance and cooperation in today's intricate and interconnected world demand a nuanced approach that transcends the traditional reliance on power dynamics. The stark inequalities between nations, often referred to in the dichotomy of the "haves" and "have-nots," pose not only a moral challenge but also a practical one for maintaining global stability and prosperity. The integration of less affluent nations into a global order that champions democracy, human rights, and free enterprise is essential, not merely as a matter of ethical principle but also for the long-term benefit and security of established powers.

The rationale for this inclusive approach is multifaceted. Firstly, a world order that privileges the interests of a select group of powerful nations over the broader international community is inherently unstable. Disparities in wealth, opportunity, and political influence can fuel discontent, conflict, and instability, which, in an interconnected global environment, can have far-reaching implications, including for those at the pinnacle of the world order. Secondly, promoting democratic values, human rights, and economic opportunity globally serves to create a more harmonious international landscape, one in which trade, investment, and cultural exchanges flourish. This not only contributes to global prosperity but also reduces the likelihood of conflict, creating a safer world for all.

Furthermore, the pressing challenges of the 21st century—such as climate change, pandemics, cyber threats, and international terrorism—do not respect national borders and cannot be effectively addressed by any single nation, regardless of its power. These issues require unprecedented levels of international cooperation, which can only be achieved through a global governance system that is perceived as legitimate and just by the majority of the world's population. This, in turn, necessitates the inclusion of diverse perspectives and the equitable distribution of both responsibilities and benefits.

However, ensuring that global institutions are "fit for purpose" in this new era is no small task. It requires a concerted effort from all stakeholders to reform existing structures, processes, and norms to better reflect the realities of a multipolar world. This involves not only opening up spaces for the participation of emerging economies and developing countries in decision-making processes but also ensuring that these institutions are capable of addressing a wide array of global issues in an effective and timely manner.

Moreover, fostering cooperation and addressing the diverse needs and concerns of the global community will require a commitment to dialogue, mutual respect, and compromise. It will involve recognizing the legitimacy of different development models and the right of nations to chart their own paths within a framework of shared values and common goals. This does not mean compromising on fundamental principles such as human rights and democratic governance but rather finding ways to support their realization that are respectful of cultural and historical differences.

In conclusion, the future of global governance lies in forging a more inclusive, equitable, and cooperative world order. This vision requires moving beyond a simplistic reliance on power and embracing a comprehensive strategy that integrates the "have-nots" into the global system. By doing so, established powers can not only fulfill a moral imperative but also enhance their own security and prosperity. Ensuring that global institutions are adapted to this task is essential for addressing the complex challenges of our times, paving the way for a more stable, prosperous, and just global community.

Chapter 10: Conclusion

Globalization, in its broadest sweep, has redrawn the contours of economies, societies, and politics around the world, knitting nations and communities closer in a dense web of economic, cultural, and political connections. This era of unprecedented integration has ushered in a plethora of benefits, catalyzing economic growth, enriching cultures through exchange and interaction, and fostering a degree of political convergence and cooperation that was previously unattainable. Yet, alongside these benefits, globalization has also unfurled a tapestry of complex challenges that defy simple solutions or unilateral approaches. The intricacies of these challenges are deeply embedded in the very fabric of globalization, emanating from the tensions between global interdependence and national interests, the disparities in economic gains, and the diffusion of cultural identities and political ideologies.

Navigating the complexities introduced by globalization necessitates a nuanced understanding of the evolving global landscape. This understanding must transcend conventional wisdom and simplistic narratives about the nature of globalization's impacts, recognizing both its potential to drive positive change and its capacity to exacerbate existing inequalities and tensions. It calls for an analytical approach that is attuned to the subtleties of how global forces interact with local contexts, shaping and reshaping economies, societies, and polities in ways that are often unpredictable and uneven.

Moreover, addressing the multifaceted challenges of globalization requires a steadfast commitment to inclusive and cooperative approaches to global governance. Such approaches must prioritize dialogue over confrontation, collaboration over competition, and consensus-building over unilateralism. They should aim to bring together a diverse array of voices, including those from the Global South, non-state actors, and marginalized communities, ensuring that the benefits of globalization are more equitably shared and its adverse impacts mitigated. This inclusivity is critical not only for fostering a sense of global solidarity but also for enhancing the legitimacy and efficacy of global governance institutions.

The imperative for cooperation extends across a range of pressing global issues, from climate change and environmental degradation to international trade disputes, from the regulation of emerging technologies to the management of migration and refugee flows. Effective responses to these issues will invariably require coordinated action, underpinned by a shared recognition of our common destiny in an increasingly interconnected world. This, in turn, demands a global governance architecture that is agile, responsive, and capable of harnessing the collective strengths and resources of the international community.

In conclusion, as the world grapples with the ramifications of globalization, the path forward lies in embracing its complexities with a keen and discerning eye. By cultivating a deep understanding of the changing global dynamics and committing to inclusive and cooperative approaches to governance, the international community can navigate the challenges of globalization. This journey, though fraught with difficulties, also offers the promise of forging a more integrated, prosperous, and harmonious world. The task at hand is not to retreat from the forces of globalization but to steer them in directions that maximize their potential for good while minimizing their capacity for harm.

Dr. David K. Ewen

www.GlobalStudiesUniversity.com

www.EnterpriseCollege.org

www.Bravehearted413.com

Globalization is Complex

How the World is Changing

Written by:

Dr. David K. Ewen

Ambassador Professor
Global Studies University
Enterprise College